'TWAS THE NIGHT BEFORE

A picture-story of the Nativity

Illustrated by
ARTHUR L. ZAPEL

Words by
RACHEL OLSON

MERIWETHER PUBLISHING LTD.
Colorado Springs, Colorado

DEDICATION

*These illustrations are for the lady artists in my family —
especially my granddaughter, Telita.*

Meriwether Publishing Ltd., Publisher
P.O. Box 7710
Colorado Springs, CO 80933

Editor: Rhonda Wray
Cover design: Arthur L. Zapel

© Copyright MCMXCIII Meriwether Publishing Ltd.
Printed in the United States of America
First Edition

Library of Congress Cataloging-in-Publication Data

Zapel, Arthur L. (Arthur Lewis), 1922 –
     'Twas the night before : a picture-story of the nativity / illustrations by
Arthur L. Zapel : words by Rachel Olson. — 1st ed.
          p.   cm.
     ISBN 0-916260-85-2
     1. Jesus Christ—Nativity—Juvenile literature.   [1. Jesus Christ—
Nativity.]   I. Olson, Rachel, 1951- .   II. Title.
BT315.2.Z36   1993
232.92—dc20   93-26740
                                                                                  CIP
                                                                                  AC

'Twas the night before Christmas
and far above earth
The angels prepared to announce
Jesus' birth.

The people of Bethlehem,
    a little town,
Were just getting ready to
    lay themselves down.

Out on a hillside, while watching their sheep
A group of young shepherds were falling asleep.

When suddenly out of the sky came a light
And an angel appeared, making everything bright!
"Fear not! For I bring you good news of great joy:
The miracle birth of a new baby boy."

He's the Messiah, and
praise be his birth
For he's come to save all
of the people on earth.

Sharing a manger with oxen and sheep
Nestled in blankets, the babe, sound asleep.

Glory to God, he's ended the strife
The Savior is here to give us new life.

After the angels delivered the news
The shepherds went searching
with no time to lose.

The shepherds returned,
praising God for his Son
They told many others
of this Holy One.

Wise men who lived
in a land far away
Saw a star burning,
like the sun in the day.

They searched for the
meaning of this brilliant light
For they'd never before
seen the heavens so bright.

They travelled the country and looked far and wide
In search of the babe - the star was their guide
Herod was furious when he heard the news
Of another king - the King of the Jews.

The angel told Joseph
to quickly take flight
So they fled off to Egypt
in the darkness of night.

Jesus taught many as he grew strong and tall.
The children flocked 'round him and he loved them all.

Now all of these things
came to pass as was told
Fulfilling the promises
God made of old.

Each Christmas we honor
the birth of God's Son
And remember the cross
where salvation was won.

We celebrate Jesus,
the Truth and the Light.
Merry Christmas to all,
and to all a good night!

ABOUT THE AUTHOR

RACHEL OLSON

Rachel and her husband, John, live with their two children in Rothschild, Wisconsin, where she teaches high school English and drama. She has been involved with children's and adult drama for 16 years in church and community theatre productions. She has two published plays to her credit. This is her first book. It is an adaptation of her very popular children's play of the same title.

ABOUT THE ILLUSTRATOR

ARTHUR L. ZAPEL

During his lifetime career as a writer/editor of plays, documentaries and advertising for radio, TV and film, Art dabbled in fine art painting. This hobby became the passion of his senior years. Now his oil paintings are sold in galleries and exhibited in major art shows in the west. Though a fine art painter and not an illustrator, Art was delighted at the opportunity to illustrate this book. He feels that it is a uniquely memorable telling of the Nativity story. He lives and works in Colorado Springs and Westcliffe, Colorado.